BASIC ON STAGE SURVIVAL GUIDE FOR AMATEUR ACTORS

Tips, Rules, And Tricks (revised)

Lee Mueller

Playedwell Publishing

PLAYEDWELL
PUBLISHING

CONTENTS

INTRODUCTION

The Basic On Stage Survival Guide is just as the title implies - a basic guide for first-time actors in any theatrical production; which could be grade school, high school, community theatre, etc...

It is written from the most basic level - as if you have **never** stepped on a stage before and have very little knowledge of the theatrical arts or traditions. But of course you are interested. You need a basic introduction.

This book covers what any new actor may expect from auditions through rehearsing a play. It introduces some basic terms you hear as well as trivial information such as where *upstage/downstage* are located. You may even learn obscure terms such as *rain rehearsals.* You may have always wondered how do those actors memorize all thos lines? Well, I will teach some great methods.

Basic On Stage Survival Guide also introduces a few

guidelines and rules of the stage. As a new actor, I learned the hard way by breaking these rules. Who knew there were rules? Such as- if it falls – pick it up. Well now you can learn the easy way.

Hopefully, most of the information in this book will help new actors (and in some cases old veterans of the stage) learn some tips and tricks and survive their first (or hundredth) theatrical experience.

-Lee Mueller

Thank you to my wife Patti for encouraging this project. I would also like to thank Arno Kracht, my high school drama teacher who first taught me the basic rules and guidelines of the stage. And to all the teachers, actors, directors, and others who have shaped me in the world of theatre and taught me survival skills for the stage many times! Raymond Keller, Diane Breitwieser, Ray Sikes and Jason Wells to name a few. A special thanks to the late great Earl Hyman whose class at HB Studios in NY taught me more in an hour than two years of acting classes anywhere.

PART 1

THE AUDITION

WHAT IS AN AUDITION?

In its simplest terms; an audition is a process where actors read from a script in front of a director or a casting committee. The director (or casting committee) will then select those actors which best fit the characters for the play.

If you've never been to an audition, you may have a picture in mind of an actor standing on a barren stage, looking out into an empty theatre and there in the distance of the darkness, you can just make out the shadow of a director. This may be the classic setting used in movies, TV shows, and maybe based on professional theatrical auditions on and off Broadway, but it's not very realistic on the amateur community theatre level.

The director sitting in the dark may be accurate for for some groups but here we will focus on the non-professional, nowhere near Broadway, extremely amateur theatre auditions. The place where most actors start.

So, having said that,(*or written that as the case may be*), let me also write - that in the world of non-professional or community theater, auditions are less dramatic. (but not necessarily the people. Spoiler: some theatre people can be very dramatic IRL.)

I have attended auditions that were held in church basements, banquet halls, high school gymnasiums, Churchs and even in someone's garage. Only on a rare occasion did I audition on a stage in an actual theatre. I am not saying you won't, just be prepared because amateur auditions can be held in very odd spaces.

The most basic (non-professional) audition is open to the public at a set time. All hopeful actors arrive and sit around in a common room or area and wait to audition. This type of audition is sometimes referred to as a "*cattle call*" because the actors are ushered in and out similar to a herd of cattle being lead from the barn to the field. Or to the slaughter house on a bad day.

Note: There are theatre groups who practice a professional approach and actually schedule auditions by appointment, similar to a job interview. At this "appointment" audition, an actor will meet with very few people and hardly any cattle. But for the sake of this topic let's assume we are attending an open non-professional, generic, community theatre audition.

❊ ❊ ❊

SO WHAT HAPPENS AT AN AUDITION?

The first thing you usually do is fill out an audition form. It's similar to job application but, instead of employment history, you will list any previous performance experience. Yes, you can list the time you played a "Tree" in the 3rd grade Arbor Day pageant.

Most directors will be interested in learning how much stage experience you have. They want to be assured you will not freeze on stage or running screaming in the middle of a play. Many directors will make a decision based on your talent, your look, and your availability. Experience is important but it isn't everything.

You may see some hopeful actors bring an acting resume or portfolio complete with 8 x 10 photos, but don't let that intimidate you, a portfolio is not a sign of talent. It's merely a sign that they have been doing this theatre thing for a while and want to appear semi-professional. I know quite a few semi-pro theatre types who still don't have portfolios. Don't worry about it yet.

Starting out – what you should worry about are schedule conflicts. An important piece of information to include on an audition form, beside your experience, are any conflicts you may have with the rehearsal schedule. This is the *Availabilty* factor. I have witness someone who was wonderful at the audition and perfect for the role, but since they would be out of town for most of the rehearsals, the role went to someone else.

 A director will let you know the rehearsal and performance time and dates before anything else. Let me warn you, directors hate schedule conflicts.

If the rehearsals are scheduled to run Tuesday through Friday evenings and you work Tuesday and Wednesday night and have classes on Thursday until 8 pm, you will want to list those conflicts. Scheduling conflicts can really influence the director's final decision. In some rare cases, a director may make an exception for an actor, but not very often. I did a production where one of the main actors could only be the first rehearsal and the last two rehearsals before opening night. An exception was made for this actor. It can happen.

Now let's get to the heart of the matter: the actual audition.

An audition is a very good place to get your feelings hurt, your ego bruised, your bubble burst, and other sorts of personal trauma. So, please keep in mind, a director is looking for a particular *type* of actor to fit a particular role.

 If the play is about a group of teenagers struggling with peer pressure, it's doubtful a director would cast older adults. Even if Robert DeNiro and Dustin Hoffman happened to be at the auditions, it's very unlikely they would get a part.

Note: Bottom line is that a director will not always choose the best actors but will choose the actors that are best for the characters in a play.

AUDITION HOMEWORK

As I said, you can get your feelings hurt if you are not chosen for a part in a play. A good way to avoid hurt is to do a little homework prior to an audition.

What kind of homework? You may ask? I may tell you - the kind where you research the play and find out exactly what *type of characters* does the play call for? This will be a strong clue as to what type of actors in which the director will be looking to cast in the roles.

In most cases, audition notices that appear in news-papers, on social media or on theatrical websites will describe the age range, body type, ethnic type, and other helpful character hints.

Here is an example of audition notice I found on-line:

Swell Summer Theatre announces open auditions for Neil Simon's comedy - *Barefoot in the Park* on **Wednesday, Feb 4, and Thursday, Feb 5, from 7:00 pm to 9:00 pm at the Community Opera House, Front Entrance (Auditions in Community Room).** No appointment is necessary. Please wear clothes and shoes you can move in and be prepared to do some improvisation and cold readings from the script with other actors. Rehearsals will take place evenings three to four times a week.

Performance dates are **FOUR** weekends, April 3 – 26. Performances are at the Community Opera House, Fridays and Saturdays at 8:00 pm and Sundays at 3:00 pm (no show Easter Sunday 04/12) .

Director Joe Smith requires an ensemble cast of 6: four men and two women. Note: all roles require excellent comedic timing and are open to any ethnicity. The roles are a follows:

Corie Bratter - Early to mid-20's

Paul Bratter - Mid to late 20's

Mrs. Banks - Late 40's to Mid-50's

Mr. Velasco - Mid-50's to Mid-60's

Telephone Man - Mid 30's to 50's
Delivery Man - Any age

As you can see, all the information you need to know is in the notice - where, when, how, and why. Even the age range of the character is listed but don't let it deter you too much, usually this *a ballpark range.* When I was still in high school, I got cast in two community theatre plays as a 50 and 60 year old man. I was 17 at the time. No I didn't look ancient at the time - they needed someone to fill in the parts and I was available. Make-up can do wonders to make a kid look like his own grandpa.

Also notice the ad lists the rehearsal and performance schedule for anyone who may be conflicted. A little research homework helps.

If a local theater is casting the *"Munchkins"* for the **Wizard of Oz** and you are 6 foot 7, you may want to look for another audition. Maybe there are auditions for **Jack And The Beanstalk** somewhere and they are looking for tall actor to play the giant. There you go!

Also note that audition notices will often tell you what "kind" of auditions they will be. As you read in the above notice, it stated there would be some "improvisation" and "cold readings" from the script.

Lets take a look at what that means because I have known some amateur actors who hyperventilate when they hear the word *Improvisation*. Relax. Breathe into a paper bag. It's not that bad. Yes, and it's actually fun! Will look at that in a little while. But first....

COLD WHAT?

A *cold* reading basically means you will *read out loud* from a script without much *(if any)* preparation. If you are familiar with the play, great! You will have an advantage and for you it will be a warm reading. If you have never heard of the play, you will have to approach it "cold". To get an idea or feel for a cold reading, pick up a book at random and turn to any page and just start reading out loud as smoothly as possible. No pausing or stumbling over words but making your reading sound as natural and as conversational as possible. Try this and you'll get the idea. Go ahead. Try it. I'll wait.

Most directors will have a few scenes already selected from the script to use for the audition. In most cases, these scenes are usually short and may only be a few pages. You may hear the term *Sides* or *Cuttings* that refer to the pages you will read from - that's just hip lingo. In other cases you may have printed page with the scene you will read from and not the actual script. This may happen if the play is new and has not been published or maybe finished.

Also know that the audition scenes will be stronger for particular characters in the play -typically for the main characters or what many refer to as the "lead: roles. Smaller or supporting roles may not have a strong scene to read and very few lines.

As an example, I was at an audition where the character I was readind for had only *one* line in the scene. Actually, it was only one word. And that word was "Yes". It's difficult to show your acting skills by saying one word. (No, I didn't get the part.)
Now some people may argue that you can pour a lot into one word, while this may be true, having a complete sentence is more apt to demonstrate your range as an actor. At an audition, saying ONE word doesn't cut it.

One other note about (some) auditions, toward the end they may ask if anyone would like to read for a part they haven't read for yet. This is your chance if you feel you didn't have an opportunity to show them what you can do or if you didn't read for the role you wanted.

I was at an audition and read for 3 different minor roles and only read for the lead role once. I asked if I could read again, but read a different scene in the play than I had read before. Sometimes the character in a play will be displaying a different emotion - maybe he or she is angry at some point and yells or is upset and cries. It doesn't hurt to ask to read a different scene. I did and I nailed it and ended up getting the part. I'm sure if I hadn't asked I would have been cast in one of the minor roles. Go ahead and ask.

* * *

PREPARING FOR THE COLD

D on't worry about "cold" reading too much. It is very likely you will get a some time to look over the script and get a feel or idea about what's going on in the scene and with the characters. (that is if you could find nothing in your research about the play - it's new or there is nothing online - who knows) And there is a chance, it may not be until you're standing there, reading out loud that you know what's happening in the play or how you should be 'acting'.

Cold Acting

When you're reading cold, your 'acting' may be a little stiff. Perhaps the character you're reading (*from the lines you have*) seems to be angry; therefore you raise your voice. Maybe your character is supposed to have a German accent, European, or some other dialect. Maybe the character is having an emotional meltdown and having a bad day. Or laughing and having a good day. Maybe just indifferent to life itself. You really won't know until you start reading. Sometimes you can get sense of what the character is going through with the first few lines.

Many directors will use the same scenes repeatedly for all of the actors reading for parts. If you're not one of the first chosen to read, you'll have an opportunity to watch others stumble through it. This will give you a few clues about what's going on in the scene and give you a few ideas about how the characters should sound.

If there are any difficult words or pronunciations; maybe there is a line in French or German, you'll have a chance to hear how you should say it. There is no shame in stopping and asking how to pronoune a word. I recall and audition where an actor keep saying the word "*Fobe*" over and over. Finally, the director stopped and told him it wasn't *Fobe* it was *Phoebe*. The girl's name.

I've watched other actors read a scene one way and then someone else take it a different way and then when I was called up to read, tried something completely new.

Example: there was a scene where a character was angry and frustrated. The other actors who read the scene yelled their lines- really exploring the anger of the character. I tried it a different way. I remembered a scene in a film where an actor--very calmly--expressed his anger. Displaying no emotion at all and the result was quite menacing. It gave me chills. I read the scene using that technique. I did not yell. I did not get the part but I felt good about the choice I made. If five actors read the same part the same way and the sixth one does something different, who will they remember?

A Little Help

A good director will describe the scenes before anyone begins reading them. It may sound something like this:

"In this scene, you're at an all-night diner. You have a massive headache and you're trying to order from the breakfast menu but had your heart set on lunch. Inside you're feeling restless yet at peace but very sad. In the scene just prior to this you were at the hospital where your favorite aunt has died. You don't know what to do, you don't want to go home yet, so you ended up here.....and action!"

In other cases, the play may be a work that is *world famous* and they take for granted that everyone knows the plot. They know the characters and there is no need to explain the scenes. But you have no idea. You've never heard of this play. It happens. That's why research is good.

Sight And Sound

Note: A director may have you read many different parts and end up casting you in a role for which you didn't read. Directors do *not* base their decision solely on *how you read*, but many times are going on *how you look.*

 I have a friend who always gets cast as the bad guy or creepy guy soley based on his natural appearance and the strange voices he can do. He loves playing those roles. He doesn't "look" or "sound" like the handsome romantic lead and he doesn't care.

On the flip side - I know a director who likes to cast *against* type. He may cast a very odd looking, menacing guy as the romantic hero and a pleasant handsome guy as the bad guy. It's similar to a bald man with the nickname *Curly* or seven foot, 350 pound guy named *Tiny.*

VARIATIONS ON A THEME

Other auditions may request you perform a short monologue prior to cold readings from the script. Not every great actor does well at cold readings therefore, performing a monologue gives those actors a chance to shine and the director a better idea of talent.

At one audition I attended, the director handed out copies of a short monologue and allowed everyone 15 minutes to memorize as much as possible. This would show the director how quickly the actors can memorize lines and what they can do with that material on very short notice.

Some auditions may have the actors participate in improvisational games or exercises. As I stated earlier, many people panic when the hear the word "improv", but don't let the idea scare you.

Directors may use improvisation to see how well certain people work together. Do you well well with others or do you work against others? Improvisational games will show these trends. Another key directors look for is how quickly an actor can think on his or her feet.

Don't let *IMPROV* scare you. Why? If you think about it, you do it everyday! Anytime in your life where you made up an excuse, stretched the truth, or lied to someone, you were doing a basic form improvisation. When you were young and you came home late, past your curfew and you told your parents some wild story to cover your tracks... you were *improvising.* We do it all the time without really thinking about it. A conversation is improv. You say Hello, how are you? to someone, they respond and the you respond... those lines are not written down in a script that you have memorized, they are coming from you. From off the top of your head!

Without adding a whole section or lesson on the art of improvisation here (*which I could easily do*) – a simple trick to remember is when you are improvising with another person are 2 key elements: 1) *don't deny and 2) always think "yes and.. "*

So, if you are improvising a scene and someone introduces a concept **don't deny** it. Take it and build upon it. Like a conversation.

Example: *"Look! There's a dinosaur behind you!"*

Your Response: *"No there isn't."*

Well, you've ended that scene haven't you? You denied.

That scene is dead because - there is **no** where to go from that point. If you deny the statement (the dinosaur's existence), which was the main subject of the scene, then all that is left is two people standing around with nothing more to say.

Don't Deny.

Instead think *"Yes and..."*

Example: *"Look! There's a dinosaur behind you!"*

Your Response: (*could be*) *I see it! You're right! And it's wearing a Fedora! He must be a tyranus hipster-saurus! "* (or something – just keep it going by thinking in your mind *yes and...*)

You don't need to actually say *"Yes, and.."* Just have it in mind for whatever your fellow actor throws at you. Directors love creative types.

The main point of improvisation for actors is to train your mind to be ready. To be *in the moment* and listening. To build upon each thing that may happen or

NOT happen. If you have a line and go blank on stage, another actor can save you by thinking "Yes and..." It also builds trust and that is very important on stage. You want them to see the dinosaur and not deny it.

Directors also consider actors that compliment each other for a specific purpose -

Example, if the script has two characters described as *"the perfect married couple"*, the director will select two actors that look good together or have certain "chemistry" with each other. In some cases, it may not be two actors which read for those roles.

I have been cast in roles that I did not read for at an audition. The director may have heard or seen something as I read for *one part* that he found ideal for a *different part.*

In high school, for whatever reason, I always got the part of the *kindly-father-type.* Maybe it was my size or my voice, but I never got to play the villain. Once I was cast in that role, I was stuck in that role.

And once I got to College, I avoided reading for the *kindly-father-type* and finally got to play other types. I got to play the villain and other things.

So, what is the take away? - well, you may display a certain quality with your voice, inflection or presence that a director is searching for- it may fit a character in the play and you may fit a role you didn't read for.

So **voice**, **volume**, **body type**, **chemistry**, **experience**, **availability** are *all* factors a director is looking for at auditions.

They have an idealized vision in mind for each character in the play and they are trying to fill this role. A director will try to come as close as they can to that vision. It's throwing darts at a dart board. You're not going to hit the target on all of them, but you may come close. There is something-- a quality, a look, a type--they are looking for. It could be you.

A Casting Side Effect

What I have seen happen, with myself and other actors, is once a director or theatre group gets familiar with you and your work, your range, your voice, type, and your reliability -- *all of those things* - the need for you to *audition* will diminish. Seriouly. You may get put into a role without showing up. You may be sitting at home and get a call and they say, "*I have a role for a twenty something bookish type neurotic urban barista, do you want it?*"

Sure.

It happens.

Now, that we have considered all the thing a director IS looking for - let's look at a few things a director is NOT looking for.

No Poem Zone

I have seen amateur actors end up in the "*no experi-ence*" pile because they give away clues of.. well, "no experience".

In some cases, first time actors present odd behaviors because they *"think"* they are acting or have some strange idea about how it all works but most of time are only acting cringey.

These behaviors jump out with red flags waving at auditions.

The first red flag is reading from a script as if it were a poem. Stop it.

Some inexperienced actors believe "acting" means speaking in an *iambic pentameter* and everything they read has a cadence of: da-DUM da-DUM da-DUM - which is fine if you are auditioning for a play written by Shakespeare.

Note: not every play was written by Shakespeare. A few other people wrote a few other things.

If you're reading from the script and have a bouncy rhythm that you can tap your foot to - again, unless it's an Elizabethan play, stop it. Put that red flag away.

A free basic acting tip: When you're reading dialogue (*modern dialogue*), a good rule of thumb is to make it sound natural. Make it sound *conversational*. Like you are having an nice normal conversation with someone.

How do I do that?

Imagine you are speaking to a friend. It's that simple. You are not in Mrs. Morris' fourth grade classroom reading a sonnet by John Donne in front of the class or reciting a limerick - if you are reading dialogue and your rhythm sounds like:

There once was a man from Bryte,

Who had a terrible fright.

He left one day,

In a relative way,

And returned the previous night.

-there is something wrong. Not with this guy from Bryte but from the way you are reading. Is this how you sound when you talk to your friends? (Maybe it is...) Do your friends look at you with strange expressions and ask *Why are you talking like that?* If you begin reading from a script and could imagine your friends questioning the way you speak - you are doing it wrong.

If you are reading from the script and it sounds bouncy or doesn't sound like a normal conversation-you should probably **stop it**.

Remember, **it's a play, not a poem**.

It most cases, the lines you are reading out loud are words in a sentence that represent a conversation between some characters.

It has always helped me, to turn to the other actor and image we are having a conversation = to NOT think of myself as a guy standing here with a script in my hand trying to read these words, but as a person talking to another person.

Imagine that you and the other actor are someplace normal. Standing outside, having lunch or dinner somewhere - anywhere other than an audition space. Forget you are holding a script. Ignore that there may be a group of peole watching you. How would you sound when you spoke if you could forget and ignore the distractions? How do you sound when you talk to other people now?

Acting has come a long way since the days of Shakespeare. If you find yourself auditioning for a role with one hand on your hip and your other hand out stretched in dramatic fashion - **stop it.**

Accidental Accenting

A nother red flag. I have heard a few *American* actors suddenly become *British* during auditions.

One actor I knew, read every part as if he were Sir Anthony Hopkins or Ian McKellen. He believed that in order to *sound like an actor*, you must use a proper English accent.

This is another call-back to believing every play is written by Shakespeare. It's not.

Now, reading a part using a British accent would be great if the part were a British character and it called for an accent or the director *asked* for an accent. But this actor, I knew - would use his accent for every role he auditioned for.

I could even imagine him using his accent when auditioning for Stanley Kowalski in "A Street Car Named Desire". *If you don't know, "Streetcar" is set in New Orleans, and sounding like it's set in Downton Abby doesn't really fit the part.*

Now of course, if you are reading this in the United Kingdom ignore everything I said above. It doesn't apply.

There is also an accent some actors use called *"Mid-Atlantic or Transatlantic "*. It was taught in many prestigious acting schools in the early 1900's and was the standard for the stage .

 It sounds like a watered down British accent that has been mixed with Upper Class American.

Many film actors of the 1930's and 1940's used the Mid-Atlantic accent. You can hear it in movies from those decades from the main star down to the extra who has one line. The Mid Atlantic accent softened hard consonants, especially the "r's".

Example: an actor would say *"ra-tha"* instead of *"rather"*.

 It was used by Katherine Hepburn, Bette Davis, and Vincent Price to name a few. It doesn't hurt to know accents, in fact, I was in a play set during the 1930's and the director wanted the actress to use Mid-Atlantic accent. She had never heard it, so it was recommended she watch old films. (Actually, a contemporary actress, Jennifer Jason Leigh, uses a Mid-Atlantic accent perfectly in the film, *The Hudsucker Proxy*.)

I have also worked with a few actors who will suddenly use an accent for only certain words. (for some odd reason) They will be moving along just fine and suddenly, roll an "r" in a word - a trait of the Mid-Atlantic accent. Or suddenly sound Irish or German while pronouncing words. The director told them to stop.

Although, I may have strongly suggested they stop as well.

Sometimes an accent can run away from you. I had to play an Irishman once and a few times my accent became Scottish.

On the other side of the spectrum, (or pond), I have heard actors suddenly sound as if they are from Brooklyn when reading for a role.

This may be a simlar case when a person thinks that actors should sound like DeNiro or Pacino.

As a side note: I could never understand why Fonzie on Happy Days had a New York accent - the show was set in Milwaukee, Wisconsin. I have a several friends from Milwaukee - they've never sounded like Fonzie.

 I have also noticed that actors on TV "Police" shows - tend to slip into a New York accent when playing a cop - even if the show is set in Chicago or elsewhere. So, I can't really blame novice actors for using the New York accent when professionals are using it for no real reason.

Bottom Line

   Again, if the roles call for an accent, fine. But, unless the character description tells you the role has an accent or the director wants you to read the part that way, clear the accents from your mind. Read the part in your own voice and accent.

* * *

Beyond the Sound Barrier

One major factor that directors look for or in this case what they actually *listen* for - is your sound.

What?

Yes, sound.

The noise coming from your face.

Do you speak loud enough to be heard or do you mumble softly to yourself?

Speech volume is very important on the stage because everyone needs to hear you. Not only your fellow actors, but all the people in the audience need to hear the words you are saying. Especially the people in the very back row. It's important to the plot of every play to hear the dialogue.

While it is true many theatres have invested in wireless sound systems these days and may wire every actor with a lavalier microphone, it's still nice to have a strong clear, loud voice - in the event the batteries go out in your power pack.

Unlike people watching T.V. at home, theater audiences do not have remote controls to adjust the volume.   Having said that, a director will look for actors with volume control and know how to turn it up, therefore it's important at an audition TO MAKE YOURSELF HEARD.

Perhaps the theatre has an amazing sound system and the stage and the actors will be wired with microphones, so it won't be an issue - but having a strong, clear voice is always a plus.

A helpful tip for having really good volume at an audition: *Don't hold the script up in front of your face when reading. Hold in down at an angle.*

 Why?

Because holding it in front of your face creates a wall or sound barrier. All of the sound coming out of your mouth hits the script and bounces back to you.

 Result: the director cannot hear you nor see your face as you speak. Besides the emotion carried in the sound of your voice, what do your eyes and face convey? It's all important. Be heard and be seen.

❊ ❊ ❊

Say What?

E nunciation is also a virtue at auditions. You may be loud enough when you read; however, you may be running all the words together into a garbled mess.

Not only must your volume be turned up, but you must be clear when you speak.

One trick is to imagine that you are speaking to an elderly person or a foreigner. We tend to speak loudly and slowly in those cases. *(Although I am not sure why people speak loudly to foreigners.)*

When I was starting out as an actor, I had a habit of swallowing the end of my sentences. What I mean is-- my volume would drop off the end of every spoken line. My amplitude would quit before the last few words came out of my mouth. A line such as:

"Hark! I hear the cannon's roar!"

 would become:

"Hark! I hear the cannon's roar!"

What? The cannon's rear?

No! Roar. ROAR.

A microphone drop is one thing but a volume drop - not so good. Especially if you are doing comedy. If the audience learns they can't hear what you are saying, they won't laugh - because it will drown you out.

A director pointed out the issue I was having with my volume. He said, listening to you is like falling off a cliff. Stop it.

Once my volume-dropping-tendency was pointed out and I became aware of it - I stopped doing it. It was my own natural cadence - here was a case of sounding too much like natural conversation. I was able to change that aspect of my normal speaking voice. I started getting more parts at auditions. And people stopped misunderstanding what I was saying in real life.

The point is: along with your volume and enunciation, it's helpful to be aware of your basic communication habits. Any odd little habits you may have, it's helpful to be aware of them and try to correct them. Do you have odd habits? Do you clear your throat for no reason after every sentence? Do you pause in mid-sentence for no real reason? Do you swallow the end of your sentences? Well, don't.

How?

Listen to yourself.

Record yourself speaking or reading and listen for any anomalies. Ask a friend, maybe they will be honest and tell you and if they tell you.. maybe you won't be friends anymore, but hey, you learned something.

 Maybe you sound as if you are asking a question even when you are making a statement. Or as I used to do, trail off at the end. Maybe you get louder at the end of your sentence. Perhaps you have no issues when you speak and that's brilliant!

In conclusion, if you are auditioning for the very first time, do a little homework and find out as much as you can about the play. The internet is a very handy tool to accomplish this task.

Also, if you are new to the acting field be careful of any set ideas you have about acting. Remember, it's a play, not a poem. No boucing.

Speak clearly, loudly and without any accent. (*unless you are supposed to - or you naturally have one*). These tips will keep you out of the "no experience" pile.

All of these methods help you look and sound good and help the director discover the best actors for the roles. Hopefully, it will be you. I'm sure it will. We're all counting on you. (no pressure)

One extra note here: many theatre groups may have

"call backs" after the initial auditions. It doesn't mean you **have** the part, it means you are in strong contention for the part.

You will have to go through the audition process one more time, (maybe more) At the **Call Back** there will be less people and everything will be a little more relaxed. You may read the same part. You might read a different part or be paired up with someone else. That doesn't mean you should relax, get sloppy and forget everything I told you. If you do. **Stop it.**

The First Cuts

A s I said a "Call Back" is essentially another audition. In some cases, there can be more than one audition.

The director may have liked a few actors who read at the *first* audition but wants to see (and hear) them read with a few actors who were at the *second* audition. They may have called someone in to the audition who is perfect for one of the parts, but they need to see/hear this actor read a scene with you.

Not everyone who auditioned will get a "call back". A callback is like the first cut for the final team. There may be second or third cuts.

Hopefully, you will make it through the auditions and call backs..

 And if you do - welcome to rehearsals.

PART 2

THE BASIC
REHEARSAL
PROCESS

READ THROUGH

One of the first things you will do in a rehearsal is called a "read-through". A read-through is just that, everyone sits around and reads throught the play. You will read it out loud. This will be one of the first times (and maybe only time*) you will *hear* the play from start to finish, word for word, as it was written.

(*Sometimes a director will cut words or lines. Yes, playwrights hate this, but it happens all the time. Also, as actors begin to memorize their lines; words or phrases may change because their recall/memory adapts, alters, and evolves during the rehearsal process. The more an actor repeats those changes, the more it becomes cemented as correct. I have gone back and re-read the script and realized I had been saying some of my lines completely wrong.)

It is during the *"read-through"* that you will get a sense of how the play sounds, how it moves *(the pace),* and how your fellow actors are going to approach their roles.

If the play is a comedy, you will get a good idea where the laughs will be. Of course, a live audience will never laugh where and when you expect it. If the play is a drama, you will learn where and when the "dramatic" moments are.

The read-through you give you a sense of *the flow* of the play. You may not get a sense of any of these elements again until the final rehearsal or the first performance because the rehearsal process chops scenes up - you may work on Act One for a week and then part of scene 3 or the end of Act Two etc...   But don't worry about that now, because the important thing is to work toward performing your role* without training wheels which is the written script.

(*A bit of trivia on the term **"role"** – which refers to the *character* you play. In the early days of theater, to save time and money, they would not give out full scripts to every actor, instead they would hand out rolled up parchment or paper that contained the actor's lines in a given scene. Why does *Spear Holder Number 2* need a full script? He just stands there and has no lines. So, an actor was given a *'role'* of paper instead of a complete script. Of course, this trivia may be completely false but it really sounds good.)

As mentioned before, the other terms you may hear when actors refer to the script or roles: a *cutting* or *sides*. Essentially, from what I can tell - cutting or sides are just the parts of the script with a particular scene.

You might hear these words at an audition -
"We'd like you to read a *cutting* from the play." or We'd like you do read *sides* with another actor."
Different regions or levels of theatre (amateur /professional) have different terms. You never know what you term for something you may hear. Unfortunately, life does not come with closed captions or translations.

YELLOW LINE GUIDE LINE

One of the first things actors do when they get a script is to highlight all of their lines on every page. Yellow is the most common color used for this practice.

Highlighting makes your lines easier to see on the page: example- if look away from your script, you can quickly glance back at the page and find your place. Having your lines stand out in yellow on a black and white page draws your eye toward it. Believe me, there is nothing more frustrating than waiting for an actor to find his place in the script.

Another fact about highlighting is that you can easily flip through the script and see which pages you have lines and those you don't. An important guideline I will suggest here and explain in detail later, is that when you highlight your lines on a page, also highlight (in a different color) the last few words of the line (or action) just before it. Knowing where and when to say your lines is important. A key that helps you is knowing who says a line before you do and knowing what they say.

❊ ❊ ❊

Blocking and the pencil Rule

After the "read through", the first rehearsals will consist of "staging" your movement; where you stand, what direction you should walk, where and when you enter and exit. Movement on a stage is commonly referred to as *"blocking."*

As you read the play you will notice that the script has "suggested" movement or blocking appearing in italics. You will see phrases such as *"walks upstage and exits"* but keep in mind, the suggested movement is only that, a suggestion.

Playwrights add very basic movement direction to give a reader an idea of what is happening or should happen on stage. If a character needs to leave the scene, the playwright will indicate this action by suggesting :*"walks upstage and exits"*.

Your actual movements - other than the general entering and exiting, will be given to you by the director.

Rule 1: Write your blocking in pencil

Yes, pencil. Why? Because directors tend to change their minds and it's very hard to erase pen.

A director may tell you to walk *Upstage* after you say your line, but at the next rehearsal has decided you should remain Downstage after you say your line. A week later realizes that walking Upstage was better.

❊ ❊ ❊

UP HERE AND DOWN THERE

One bit of stage trivia I learned from a theater history major was the origin of stage areas: **upstage** and **downstage**. (*Note: I don't know how factual this information is -but I always found it helpful because it created an imagine in my mind*)

The story goes: Once upon a time - in the early days of theater, the space where the audience sat was a flat, level area. This of course made it difficult for people sitting in the back, or even a few rows back, to see all the action up on the stage. To make it easier for the audience to see, the stage was built on an incline that went up toward the back, sort of like a ramp.

An actor standing at the very back of the stage was slightly higher "up" than anyone at the front of the stage. This angle made it easier for the audience to see everything and everyone on the stage. Hence, we have the terms

UPSTAGE - meaning the back of the stage and
DOWNSTAGE which means the front.

To move "upstage" an actor was walking "up the stage" toward the back and moving "downstage" was walking "down the stage" to the front. This bit of trivia, made it much easier for me to remember the ups and downs of stage directions.

Many times platforms or risers are used on the stage to highlight different levels or designate areas which will be up and down.

As an example: a script may call for the front of the stage to represent the front yard of a home. Just beyond this "yard" area will be a porch and then the interior of a house. The stage designers may use a platform for the house interior to distinguish a different area on stage.

 Perhaps inside the house (the set) there will be a set of stairs leading up to a second story, another platform or riser will be used to represent the upstairs area. Everything on the stage starts "down" at the front and gradually moves "up" toward the back of the stage.

One Exception to this: there is something called *Theatre in the Round.* For many years I worked at a playhouse in St. Louis that was just that - theatre in the round. It was a small stage, surrounded on four sides by the audience. The stage was essentially was down in a pit and the audience sat in four different sections that rose at a 45 degree angle above from the stage area. There was no real upstage or downstage for the actors - for the audience yes, but no one else. The plays that were performed had rarely had set - mostly they used furniture pieces to represent the set.

The actors had to play to all sides since they were visable on all sides. Stage directions for this type of theatre can vary from a clock configuration, meaning upstage is 12:00 and downstage would be 6:00 etc.. Stage Right is 9:00 and Stage Left is 3:00.

Novice Note: Stage Right and Stage Left are from the actor's point of view. (in a normal style stage)

No trivia is provided for right and left. I will assume you can figure that out.

Rule 2: Don't Upstage

There is also a term you may hear called "*upstaging*", but this quite different than "up stage" explained before.

This "***upstage***" is not a place or direction but an *action*. The action of "upstaging" means to steal attention or focus away from another actor.

Example: if you stand directly in front of another actor, blocking the audience's view, you are "upstaging" that actor. Since you are standing in front of - or *downstage* of the actor, you have moved the actor *upstage-* where the audience cannot see him.

You may have seen old comedy routines or musical numbers where one actor or singer butts in front of another to 'steal the spotlight' - this is called "upstaging".

Directors, (generally) will make sure none of the "blocking" they give you, will create upstaging. It's highly unlikely you will be told to enter the scene and stand in front of another actor. Unless, it's for effect.

An important note: *Upstaging* is a very good concept to be aware of as an actor. If you ever find yourself standing in front of another actor, you should know something is not right. What's not right is you are breaking the rule that says "**Don't upstage**".

Now, this is the most basic form of upstaging because it is quite literally a physcial *action*. So, we can say in this form "upstage" becomes a verb. And you may hear that verb many times by actors and directors.

Hint: it will usually haved the *-ing* suffix "upstaging" so, you will know it's *not* the area of the stage.

In the next part, the action of upstaging takes on

more meaning but it helps to understand that many directors work hard to make an audience "look" where they want them to look.

How?
They use lighting, blocking, and all types of visual elements to say to the audience: *"Pay attention to this area right here. I need you to see **this** because something important is happening."*

Directors really appreciate it when an actor doesn't destroy the visuals they create and make the audience look away from where they need to be looking.

The downstage right area may have special lighting for a special scene. It may be brighter than the rest of the stage. The focus of the audience will naturally be directed to this area. In this special bright light, two actors are playing out a crucial love scene. But then an actor on the other part of the stage, in the darker area, (not involved in the scene), begins moving around or making noise. The audience's focus will now be directed to this other actor - because.... he is *stealing* the focus. Which is almost the same as standing right in front of the actors in the love scene. Which is - you guessed it -called *Upstaging*. Let's explore this. Focus on the next page.

LOOK AT ME!

The term *upstaging* can also refer to the act of "stealing focus". To recap: *Stealing focus* is simply calling attention to yourself in some manner, or making the audience look at you instead of where they should be looking.

Example: If another actor is speaking on stage and you suddenly begin jumping up and down or maybe just fall down and play dead, odds are - the audience will look at you. This is called "upstaging".

You are destroying the visual the director tried to achieve. Maybe it's the crucial scene where the detective finds a key piece of evidence or Caesar is stabbed but the audience didn't see it because an actor on far stage left decided to tie his shoe. That simple movement of tying a shoe stole the audience's attention.

There are many forms of *upstaging* that do not involve standing in front of someone or drawing attention with sudden movement. Upstaging can be subtle.

Example: During a play, an actor and I had a scene involving a dramatic conversation. The director had blocked ups to play this scene downstage center. Just behind us, or slightly "upstage" , were three other actors who were supposed to be silently, listening to our conversation.

(that was the direction the director gave them - You three actors - stand there silenty and listen - it was written into their scripts with pencil)

Each night during this scene, I could hear giggles and snickering from the audience. The scene was very serious; there was nothing remotely funny about our dialogue, therefore, I couldn't understand why people were laughing. Was I or the other actor doing something? Mispronouncing a word, or maybe someone's fly was open?

One night, during that scene, out of the corner of my eye, I saw exactly the reason for the giggles. One of the actors behind us, was being overly *animated* in his role of "*listening*". By animated, I mean he was shaking his head in agreement with some of our lines and making large sad faces and wiping his eyes during dramatic lines. Because this actor's actions were so cartoon-ish or over the top, the audience's attention or focus was drawn to him. His melodramatic acting did not fit the mood of the scene and as a result it caused people to laugh.

The actor wasn't intentionally trying to make anyone laugh; he honestly thought he was contributing to the scene, he thought he was *acting* but, in reality, he was "*upstaging*".

It should also be noted that getting a laugh from the crowd can be addicting. Sometimes actors find that if they do little things, gestures etc.. and the audience reacts, they will keep doing it, whether they are upstaging or not.

You may get a small role in a play such as *crowd person number 2* and invite all your friends and family to come and see the play. Naturally, you want everyone to see you in the crowd scene. You will want to stand out in the crowd. But unless you are in a grade school production, waving to your friends and your mom isn't really necessary. Sure, everyone will see you, but you'll be doing what? Yes! Upstaging! Stop it.

 Unless of course, everyone else in the crowd scene is also waving to their mom – if that is the case, then don't worry about it. Wave away!

Side Note: I was cast as an extra in a movie *(Escape From New York)* and was in a scene where a group of crazy people came out of the sewers and chased the hero down the street. Our costumes were layers of burlap sacks and we all looked the same. The scene was shot at night, it was raining, and I knew there would be *no way* to tell which one of the crazy burlap sacks guys was me. Unless I did something different - not upstaging - but just so I would be able to tell which one was me. When we began shooting the scene, (I recall we may have done five takes) - as we ran down the street, I would stay stage left (Or screen left) for every shot.

Now, when the movie plays on TV, I can point to the burlap sack on the right side of the screen and say, "That's me right there." Granted, this has nothing to do with theatre but it does have to do with a way to make yourself known in a crowd scene without stealing focus.

So Rule: Don't upstage by standing in front of another actor. Don't steal focus by jumping up and down, waving to your mom**,** or any movements, gestures or actions that may take the audience's attention.

❊ ❊ ❊

Initial Direction Details

You may have a detailed director and find yourself writing down your blocking (stage directions) all over your script; in the margins, on the top, on the bottom, anywhere you can find blank spaces.

It's important to get the director's details and blocking down the first time. Directors really get annoyed when they have to repeat directions over and over. Your script may end up looking a little like this:

TROY: I must ~~leave~~ you now.   *[SAD] [TURN RIGHT]*

HELEN: Leave? Now? Why? *) CROSS DL*

TROY: There's too many places *[STRONG]*
I've got to see!
— BEGIN CROSSING UR - TURN

HELEN: Whatever.

TROY: Good bye Helen. *[BRAVE] PAUSE / TURN*
EXIT

It may look like "chicken scratch" to anyone else but hopefully, it will make sense to you. Some actors write very long and detailed notes in their scripts while others such as myself, essentially make caveman drawings. As long as you understand what the director wants you to do - where you should stand, walk etc.. that is what is most important.

This is where we can start going a little deeper into the process and I can share some helpful hints or short-cuts I have learned from other actors. It should be said - different actors have different methods of doing things - most of these are what I gathered from others - you can use them or adapt them into your own. So, enough of this banter...

Let me share a few tips and short cuts you can use to write down your blocking.

Baby Steps

At first, the director may give you very basic directions such as:

"Come in through the upstage right doorway and cross to down center."

Instead of writing it word for word, it's helpful to abbreviate directions like *"cross to down center"* with *"cross DC"* and *"walk downstage right"* with *"walk DR"*.

You can just use the first letter of each area of the stage:

U = Upstage   **D** = Downstage

C = Centerstage   **R** = Right and **L** = Left.

As you may have noted from the example above you can combine letters or mix and match: DC -Downstage Center, UR -upstage Right, etc...

I know a few actors who abbreviate the action of "crossing" or "cross" with an "X". So, if the blocking is: "cross to upstage left" you can write "X-UL".

I have even used arrows as shorthand to save space in my script. I am standing centerstage and the director tells me after I say my line, cross stage right: I will write an X for cross and an arrow pointing left or right.   <----   I will know that it means *Cross to the Right*.

Bigger Steps

As the rehearsals progress, the director may add more detail to the basic directions he or she first gave you, such as:

"When you enter the upstage right door and cross down center, I want you to look around the room as you cross. This is the first time you've been in this room and it's all new to you. And as you look around, be a little curious. Have a curious look on your face."

You can either write it out; "look curious when crossing down center" in your script, or simply write "*curious*" next to "X DC ". (*cross down center*)

The point is, as long as you know what it means, that's all that matters. Don't worry if you forget, I have spent minutes I will never get back waiting for an actor who is trying to read his own writing and can't remember where he is supposed to be.

Now there are a few rules you must know while you are *X-ing DC* and *Exiting UR.*   These rules apply to what you should and should not do, in the same catagory as the Upstage verb.

That's Cheating!

A term you will learn during blocking is *Cheating*. This does not mean copying your stage directions from another actor's script, it means "turning slightly toward the audience."

There may be a scene where your character will be talking to another character and the director will tell you to "cheat." or "cheat out". In real everyday life, humans tend to face one another when talking:

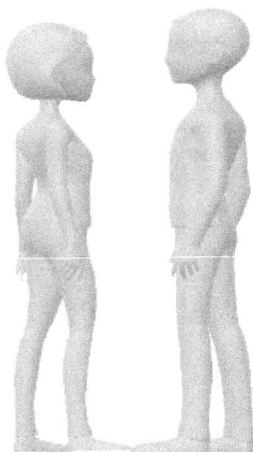

However, on the stage, it's bad karma to turn away or not face the audience. After all, they paid good money to see the play and they are entitled to see a whole face, not just the side. You're cheating the audience.

(O.K. that isn't the real reason. It really has to do with 'sound' -more later)

If you do turn to talk, like a normal human, the director may tell you to "cheat" toward the audience. Because, well, it's a rule.

Rule 3: Cheat Toward the Audience

To "cheat" or "cheat out" means to angle yourself toward the audience and slightly away from the actor you are speaking to on stage.

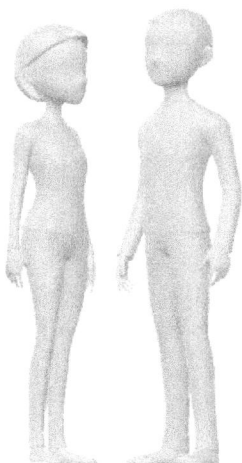

At first, when you have to 'cheat' toward the audience, it will feel awkward and unnatural but, it will make the director and the audience happy.

To make it feel less awkward, imagine you're standing

around and someone with really bad breath walks up and starts talking to you. They just ate a sandwich of raw garlic, sardines, and limburger cheese. You really don't want to be in the path of the stink breath, so you turn slightly away to allow some good air to filter in. That is what "cheating" on the stage is like.

Another "cheat"--that may feel awkward--is delivering your lines to an actor who is standing behind you. If you think the audience gets insulted when you turn sideways, imagine how enraged they would be if you turned your back on them.

Rule 4: Never turn your back on the audience.

Why? Well, if they throw something, you won't see it coming. O.K. not totally true. But most directors will have a fit if you turn your back on the audience. Now, there are always exceptions - sometimes a director will have you turn your back or turn sideways for dramatic effect. This rule of course, only applies to an actor that is speaking.

If you need to exit the stage and the doorway is upstage, you will, of course, turn and walk upstage to exit -in this case, your back will be to the audience which is perfectly natural. More natural than taking this rule literally, and trying to exit upstage by walking backward.

If you need to exit upstage but have a few lines to deliver, the common practice is to start your cross upstage, stop and turn back to deliver your lines, and then continue to your exit.

Cheat Talking

If you are standing downstage and someone enters upstage (which of course, will be *behind* you), and you have to deliver lines, you will "cheat" by saying your lines either slightly turned or facing straight ahead.

I have heard many explanations of the "cheating" rule, but the one that makes the most sense to me, has to do with *sound*.

When you are facing forward on the stage and speaking, the sound of your voice, or your "sound waves" are pointed right at the audience. They should have no problem hearing you and your waves.

Now, if you were to turn to the side or completely around, your voice (sound waves) is (are) pointed away from the audience. These sound waves will bounce around the stage and off the walls before making it out to the audience. All this bouncing brings your voice volume down a few notches and makes it harder to hear you.

Therefore, when you cheat toward the audience, you get less bounce and more volume. (It's like a great shampoo and conditioner.) Now having said that, this "sound" explaination doesn't really fit in modern times in which actors wear microphones. It doesn't matter which way they are facing, the sound is being picked up and transmitted over speakers. Heck, an actor could whisper his or her lines and it would be fine. So, as you see, some of these rules were made to accommodate a funtion, in this case "spoken sound from the stage" that in some cases doesn't apply any-more. But until this rule is voted down we will keep observing it for now.

❃ ❃ ❃

SOUND ADVICE

Another term you will hear (as well as a rule you must follow) is "Projection". As in "project!" your voice (a verb). Not to be confused with *project* as in: "Can you help me with my science project?"(a noun)

Rule 5: Project Your Voice   (if you are not wearing a microphone)

"Project" means to speak louder. Let's go back to being a normal human again: when you're talking to someone who's standing a few feet away, you'll naturally speak at a normal volume level. Now, imagine there's another person, a third person who is twenty feet away. If you're still talking at a normal volume level, chances are this third person won't be able to hear you.

 When you're an actor on a stage, (*not a normal human*) the audience is that *third person* who's twenty feet away. It's important they hear you. Again, they paid good money, not only to see your whole face but to hear the stuff you are saying.

For the newbie actor, the first time you try to project, you will feel like you are shouting, but trust me, by the time your voice (sound waves) reach the ears of people sitting twenty feet or more away, it will sound normal.

From The Gut

You may hear a director tell you to "project from your *diaphragm*." (Your diaphragm is a thin sheet of muscle under the lungs that functions with your breathing).

To project from your diaphragm means: instead of speaking from your throat, or head voice, you need to speak from your stomach.

How?
You push air up from your stomach region which gives your voice quite a boost. You can be quite loud when you speak from your diaphragm. It's like turning your voice up to 11.

Most singers know all about projecting from the diaphragm, if you know someone who sings, they can teach you.

I've known a few actors who couldn't get the hang of 'projecting from the diaphragm', so don't worry if you don't get it right away.

I knew an actor who was having a hard time understanding how to crank up his volume from the diaphragm. One day, he was imitating Pee Wee Herman and doing Pee Wee's famous laugh. (if you are not familiar with Pee Wee Herman you can find a clip on the internet)

As you may know, Pee Wee's laugh was very distinctive, very deep and loud. The reason it was loud, is because it came from the diaphragm. So, I said to the actor,

ME: "You know, when you do the Pee Wee laugh, you are using your diaphragm. "

ACTOR: "I am?"

ME: "Yea! That sound is coming up from your stomach. So, when you're on stage, just remember how you do that laugh and do the same thing with your voice. "

Another example is Death Metal. No, not the music but the growling vocal style. They are pushing air up from their stomach to get the sound to roll across their vocal chords.

✳ ✳ ✳

PRETTY PICTURES

Let's move from the world of sound to the world of sight. When directors design "blocking" for the stage, they attempt to create interesting images for the audience to see. Careful thought and planning go into where the actor stands and where they move etc..

 Example: If there are 3 or 4 people on the stage and they're all standing in straight line, similar to a police line up, it's not very interesting. In fact, it's downright dull. Unlike television or the movie screen, the stage has 3 dimensions. It has depth. That's 3-D with no special glasses needed.

The Triangle Principle

Many directors use the triangle principle. The triangle principle states that if there are 3 actors on stage, they should be spaced to form a triangle. One actor maybe standing a few feet upstage and the second actor is a foot downstage and so forth. If you were on the ceiling of the stage looking straight down, they would form a triangle.

 The basic idea is to have actors spaced at different

depths on the stage and avoid straight lines. It's much more interesting to look at from the audience's perspective.   A director may also ask you to "counter."

Rule 6: Don't Stand In A Line - create depth- Make A Triangle

If you are standing on the stage and one or two others actors move toward you in a scene, you should "counter," which means take a step back or forward to create a triangle. Even after weeks of rehearsal, some actors may forget and stand right next to you on the stage. In that case take a step to counter.

Don't worry - it will look natural if you take a step forward or backward.

Picture Psychology

There are some directors who follow the psychological areas of the stage. Yes, that's what I said. There are some areas of the stage that are "stronger" than other areas. What makes them stronger? Well, you see most people tend to view images from left to right. That is how you are reading this; you started on the left side and ended on the right. Our brains are wired from left to right, unless of course, this is translated into an Asian language then it would be up and down, or others who read right to left, but the point is the American/European eye is trained to view things starting at the left and then over to the right.

If the curtain opened on a play and all the furniture

were on the right side of the stage and all the actors were standing around it, and the left side of the stage was empty, the theory is that the audience gets an uneasy feeling from this display. As their eyes scan left to right, everything is piled up on one side and there is no visual balance on the left which causes an off kilter feeling.

Many directors will balance out the stage starting on the left and work to the right. Actors will be placed in areas that balance the stage. Since the audience starts "reading" from the left, the "downstage right" is the strongest area of the stage.

Note: *Downstage right* to the actor is actually the left side of the stage for the audience.

Many dramatic monologues or emotional scenes are staged in the downstage right area, because that's is the left side or visual starting point for the viewer and "downstage" is up close and personal.

Finally, once all of your blocking is set, your cheating is done and your volume is adjusted, you will begin running through the play over and over.

Depending upon your rehearsal schedule, you may get to run the play numerous times with the script in your hand but there will come a time when the director will want you to be "**Off Book**".

Novice Note: *Off book* means you have memorized all of your lines and blocking.

I can't stress this enough: the faster you get 'off book'

the better, because the more chances you have to speak your lines from memory, the deeper your concentration will become. But first, let's get you *off* book.

❄ ❄ ❄

PART 3

THE LINES

HOW DO I LEARN LINES?

(Some Memory Tips and Tricks)

Rule: 7 Know Your Lines

I am often asked, "what is the best way to memor-ize lines?" I don't know if there is a "best" way but I can suggest a few methods, tips and tricks I have learned over the years.

But first, if you'll recall, under the subject of "high-lighting" your lines, I mentioned it was good practice to highlight the lines or actions just *before* your lines. Case in point: I was in a play with an amateur actor who highlighted all of his lines and memorized them, so we all could see how dedicated he was.

The rehearsal began and our dedicated actor an-nounced he could function off book because he had all of the lines down cold. So, we began running through the play and what do you know - our dedicated actor was completely lost. Why? Yes, he knew his lines; however, he didn't know "when" to say them. He hadn't dedicated himself to memorize his "cues" along with his lines. What's a cue? A cue is the line or action that prompts your line.

Example:

PERSON 1: How are you today?

PERSON 2: I'm just fine! How about you?

If you are *Person 2,* the only way to know when to respond to Person 1, is by knowing what Person 1's is going to ask you.

Not only must you know your own lines, but you must also know the lines that "cue" your lines. The lines that come before your lines are your cues. That is why I suggested highlighting your cues in another color because you will need to know them. I suggest 'another color' to prevent you from accidentally reading those lines in rehearsals because it will happen. I've done it.

Rule 8: Know your cues

Ready Set Action
Another Cue Example:

The wind blows through the open window and extinguishes the burning candle.

PERSON IN THE DARK: Oh great! The candle went out!

Here you are "Person In The Dark" and as you can see, your cue is not a line that is spoken or any kind of sound you will hear, it will be something you "see." It's a cue based on an action. One of the hardest things to remember is a cue from some type of action or effect.

In most cases, the actual "*wind blowing through the window extinguishing the candle*" will not actually happen until the "Tech Rehearsals."

Novice Note: "Tech Rehearsals" (Technical Rehearsals) are usually the final week of rehearsals. This is where the all the lighting cues, sound cues and other effects (wind and candles) are worked out.

Until you get to tech rehearsal, hopefully, someone will follow along in the script and read any "action" cues out loud so you will be aware of them. I have spent what seemed like hours on stage in a rehearsal waiting for someone to say a line only to find out it was an action cue.

It's a good idea to be familiar with the lines leading up to any kind of action whether it's a lighting change or sound effect etc.. For instance, going back to the candle being blown out by the wind, if the line just before the action is - "My! It sure looks windy out there!" You may want to be aware of that line and know *a wind* is about the blow the candle out –which is your cue.

Hi, How Are You?

OK. Now that I've made you aware of *what* to memorize, let's get back to methods to help you memorize.

The first thing many actors do is the read the script a few times. Next step is to re-read the scenes you are in - those will be the pages with lines highlighted in yellow.

While you are re-reading these scenes, look for easy parts to remember, such as responding to questions.

Another character asks:
"How are you today?"
and your line is *"Just fine."*
Or they ask *"Where did you put the gun?"*

and your line is- *"I threw it in the river."*

It's a call and response. Question and Answer
In lines such as these, your *cue* is a question and you
simply *respond.* Responses to questions are easy to remember, aren't they? (Yes, they are.)
These will be the first lines you memorize.

Another trick is to pay attention to the ***subject***
of the line just before your line. Look for clues
or easy prompts. In many cases, your cue
line will contain a word or idea that relates to your
line.

Example:
SALLY: The trees look oh so lovely in fall.
DICK: Yes they do. I must get wood for the fire.

In this case, the cue for Dick's line is relative to Sally's
line. The subject of her line is "trees." Dick responds to
her statement and then seems to begin a new subject
about "wood for the fire," but we can see it's the idea
of "trees" that cue "wood." This is what I refer to as
Cue /Clues: A subject in one line relates to the thought
in the next. Cue/Clues are also easy to remember.

Once you search your script for easy Question/Answer lines and Cue/Clues you can move on to other advanced memory games.

PICTURE THIS

I n my early days on the stage, I was given a great technique that I still use today. It's very similar to the Cue/Clue example I cited above of relating one subject to another. I was a novice actor in a fairly large role and I was having trouble with a short monologue because I had to rattle off a list of items. Lists can be difficult to remember. One of the actors took me aside and suggested I tried to visualize each item in the "list" and mentally connect it or relate it to the next item.

Example:

GEORGE: When I was a kid I had a bicycle, a wagon, a dog and a purple umbrella.

The actor advised picturing each item as one image instead of trying to remember one item followed by another as in a list. The key word here is "picture." If you can see images in your mind, instead of a list of words, it makes it much easier to recall from memory.

In the example above, the list is a bicycle, a wagon, a dog and a purple umbrella. I pictured myself as "a kid" riding a *bicycle*. And the bicycle was pulling a *wagon*. And in the wagon was a *dog*. And since I didn't want to ride too fast, there was a *purple umbrella* on the back of the wagon to act as a parachute. One picture of many items related together instead of a list of words on paper.

Connect the Dots

I have used this method of "picturing" to help me memorize ever since, especially long monologues. Most monologues contain "ideas" such as Hamlet's famous soliloquy which begins "To be or not to be."

 The main idea in the soliloquy is "death" and Shakespeare uses different metaphors (images) to express Hamlet's basic question about life and death. Seeing the images can make memorization a lot easier.

The way most monologues are written, the character's subject is made up of connected ideas; this idea leads to *that* idea and the structure similar to a list. A list of ideas or thoughts instead of things. The kid riding the bicycle (first idea) that's pulling a wagon (second idea) and so on.

In Hamlet's *"to be or not to be"* speech: the subject of course is death. The very first idea is the question of " *to be*" or *"not to be"* (living or not living). This leads to the next image of "*slings and arrows*" and then to "t*ake arms against a sea of troubles*".   Since you know the main subject is death, you can relate the images of "s*lings and arrows*", which of cause death. And "*take arms*" which are weapons, again it relates back to death.   Or you can picture *arrows* flying out into the *sea* or whatever image you would like to help you build up the list of ideas.

Pretzel Safe Diamond Peanuts

Sometimes, a script may seem to have lines that present ideas that don't seem to be connected to anything. You may have a scene between 2 or 3 characters and they are all talking about 2 or 3 different things.

Example: I was in a play where a husband and wife arrive at a home and each character's lines are on a different subject. The wife's dialogue is only related to the furnishings of the house while the husband is complaining about how hungry he is, at least two pages of dialogue between two people that had no real connection or ideas relating to each other, two different subjects with no easy question/answers or Cue/Clues. I simply created mental images cues which were triggered or by the wife's unrelated lines.

Example:

WIFE: I bet she keeps all her jewels in a safe!

HUSBAND: I can't get this pretzel bag open!

WIFE: She has a dozen real diamonds you know!

HUSBAND: These peanuts are unsalted! Who buys unsalted peanuts?!

Based on the Wife's line about "jewels in a safe", I needed something to cue my line; "can't get this pretzel bag open".

So, I thought about an image of "jewels in a safe" and connected it with "pretzels" in "bag".

The jewels are locked away in a safe and you cannot open a safe. The pretzels are in a bag. I can't open the bag.

For the next line, I visually connected "a dozen real diamonds " to "peanuts are unsalted!"

Diamonds are clear crystal objects. Salt is a clear crystal object. The simple association of "diamonds" + "salt" worked as a cue for my line.

Sometimes if the cues or images are not in the lines, you must invent your own.

Between The Lines

Another method I have used to memorize lines is a tape recorder -(this was quite a while back) I would record myself reading the cue lines followed by my own lines. I then listen to the tape over and over, while I'm driving or working or whatever.

Much in the same way you learn the words to a popular song or a commercial jingle from hearing it over and over. (Repetition is the key. Repetition is the key.)

After listening to that tape for a while, I would make another tape of myself only reading the "cue" lines and allowing the tape to be blank where my line is spoken. Then when I play the tape, I would say my lines from memory during the blank spaces.

These days, you can get a digital recorder or record voice memo on your phone and that will work just like the old cassette tape recorder I used.

UNDER COVER

Another method is to simply read the script and cover up your lines with a piece of paper. As you come to your cue line, (which is highlighted in a different color) say your line out loud from memory. You can then move the paper to see how close you were to knowing the line.

You're Out of Order

When I say "close", what I mean is - as you begin committing your lines to memory, you will remember the gist of the line.

If the line is:

"Joe and me are going out for awhile, I'll pick up the ransom money on the way back. I'll see you later."

At first, you retain key phrases or clumps of words such as: *"going out"*, *"picking up ransom money"*, *"way back"* and *"see you later* .

Rarely at first, will you recall the line in the exact order as it appears on the page. You may recite it from memory as:

 "See you later. I'm going out for a while with Joe. On the way back, I'll pick up the ransom money."

You've got all the key phrases, but in the wrong order. Welcome to the wonderful world of paraphrasing! Don't worry, we all do it at first – but try not to make it a habit.

Why?

Because problems can occur if you continue to para-phrase right into the performances - those lines may be someone else's cue. Another actor may have committed to memory the last line or last few words you deliver as his cue and if you paraphrase or jumble the order of your words, it can make it difficult for every-one else. As an example – in the ransom line from before:

"I'll pick up the ransom money on the way back. I'll see you later."

'I'll see you later' may be a cue for another actor, but if it's the first thing you say instead of the last thing, it may cause the other actor severe trauma.

 One of my favorite personal examples of the para-phrase fallout came during a performance I was in of the play *"You Can't Take It With You"*.

An actress playing the part of a Russian Countess never said her lines the same way twice which made it difficult for another actor, who relied on her lines to cue his one and only line. He developed a strategy to simply wait until she stopped speaking to say his one big line: "I'll make sure you're on time, your Highness."

He would say his line regardless of what she said, because he knew it came directly after her line, so when he heard a reasonable amount of silence, he knew she was done and that was his cue.

 One night, for some strange reason, the actress said her line exactly as it was written in the script. Hearing his cue as it was meant to be, caused some type of malfunction in the actor's mind and after a slight pause, his line came out; "I'll make sure you're on *hime* your *tiness*".

Realizing what he just said, his eyes got very wide and literally his body jerked with a shock. *(Some day I may write a chapter on how to suppress laughter on stage.)*

So, be careful of paraphrasing your lines.

The Write Thing

I know an actor who approaches memorization, like studying for a final exam. He will sit at a table and read his lines over and over. He will then test himself by closing his script, taking a piece of paper and pen and writing his lines down from memory. He will then check the script to see if he made any mistakes. He does it over and over until it sinks into his memory. Rarely does he paraphrase.

Read To Me

A common method which is probably the most popular, is to find someone willing to follow along in the script and feed you your cue lines. They read from the script while you squirm and struggle to recall your lines uttering phrases such as: "No, don't tell me! I know this! This is where I say something about the thing..... OK! How does the line go?" Having a somewhat impartial person to help you can... well, help you. If you say your line incorrectly or paraphrase they will more than willing to correct you.

Pause Turn Page

Some actors I've known simply memorize their script with no special methods or outside help except a photographic memory. They can actually visualize pages of the script in their mind. I knew one such actress who, during her performance, would pause at odd times. Right in the middle of a line, she would place a beat (*novice note: Beat - pause of about one second*) for no real reason. I later found out that each pause she took corresponded to a place where her line was continued on the next page. Essentially, those odd pauses she took , were the places she mentally turned the page.

Memory Cement Blocks

Allow me to tie this all back into the process of rehearsal because this is where your memory will be tested. You can listen to your lines on tape or recite them with a friend but it is not until you're in rehearsal that all your work finally develops and begins to click and stick into place. In a rehearsal, you are hearing your cue lines from the actual actors who be saying them. Also as you rehearse you will be moving around the stage with your blocking which can really cement the lines into your memory.

Move Speak Move

You will discover that your movement/blocking will attach itself to your memorized lines. I discovered how deep this "movement = line" connection was during a line blitz.

Novice Note: A "Line Blitz" or "line rehearsal" is usually a panic session the director calls for when a play is about to open. The actors sit around and simply run all the lines from the play, no acting, no blocking, just dialogue. Sometimes, you are asked to run all the lines as quickly as possible.

Extra Trivial Note: I've also heard this referred to as a "Rain Rehearsal". The story goes that if there was bad weather during a performance, there may be a chance the power would go out. If the power went out, the audience would want their money back. But, technically, if the play was beyond the half-way point, the theater did NOT have to issue refunds since the audience saw more than half of the show. To prepare for this, actors would have "Rain Rehearsals" which was a 'speed metal' version of the play.

So, during a line rehearsal, line blitz, rain rehearsal, whatever, we were sitting around running our lines. I noticed as I was sitting there, I was having a very hard time recalling my lines. Sure I heard my cues, but the words that followed weren't entering my mind as they normally did in rehearsal.

In frustration, I got up and began pacing. As I walked around, I noticed I was picking up my cues faster and having no trouble with recalling my lines. Why?

My blocking! I realized how much of my memory of the lines were embedded in my blocking. When I say *this* line, I'm standing by the door. And for *that* line, I'm walking to the table. Not only can a someone else's line prompt you, but so can your own movement or location on the stage.

❋ ❋ ❋

GETTING INTO
A CHARACTER

As you memorize your lines and rehearse the play, you will begin to developed your "character". Character is, of course, is the "part" you are playing. Keep in mind that when you are *in a play*, you are *in a character*.

In character means you are Hamlet, Willy Loman or Spear Carrier number 2, you are not (insert your name here).

Many actors will tell you they don't really get a feeling for their character until they put on the costume and makeup.

When you begin to look like someone else and dress like someone else, well yeah, you feel like someone else. Like a character.

What's his Face

Yes guys, you will have to wear makeup but relax, it's for a very good reason. Under the bright lights of the stage, your face washes out into a blur of nothingness. If you have ever seen a photograph of someone that was taken with a very bright flash, you can sort of see the shape of a head but the face looks like a shiny bright orb, this is what stage lighting can do to your face.

To prevent you from having shiny bright orb face, you will wear a "base" or "foundation" make up that gives your face color and removes the "shiny" factor. Also, you may wear liner to define your eyes so that they show up on your face. Believe it or not many rock stars, movie and TV personalities use eye liner and foundation makeup because they are under the same type of lighting.

If you are playing an old character, you will have "age lines" or wrinkles drawn on your face and gray tinted spray will be used on your hair to make you look older.

A note about stage make up: you may notice that the first time you stand near your fellow actors, the eye liner, foundation, and old age lines will look very over-done or fake, but keep in mind the audience will not be standing next to you. The farther away you stand, the less overdone and more natural it will appear.

If you look at a painting from about an inch away from the canvas, all you can see are globs of colors smooshed together. If you move farther back from the painting, you will see those globs are actually objects that make up a picture. It's the same principle with character makeup.

Someone Else

When you have makeup on your face and you're dressed in a costume, you may begin feeling different. That's normal. Saying your lines in your everyday clothes at rehearsal is no big deal, but saying your lines in a costume will give you a new feeling. You may be feeling like someone else and that other person is your character.

If the play is set in a different time period like the 1800's or 1920's, you will be wearing older style clothes and shoes and maybe a hat. Just wearing different clothes will make you feel different. And that is the point of playing a character, a character is someone different.

Although *you know* the person on the stage is only you in a costume and makeup but keep in mind, it is not *supposed to be you*. The words you are speaking are not your own words, nor is the play a representation of your life. I say this because I have known actors who get confused by this fact.

Example: I was in a play with a girl who absolutely refused to wear her costume. When the director asked her "why?" she replied. "I would never wear colors like that! They don't even match!" He replied, "You aren't wearing those colors! Your character is!"

A final note about the character you are playing. First and foremost the director will have final say on how your character turns out. You may have a feel for the character but the director will guide you. They may to tell you to be more forceful or less forceful when saying this line or that line. You are a lump of clay they are trying to mold into something: a character in a play.

Sometimes a director may give you something that is called a *line reading.* If they believe you don't understand what you are saying, or maybe you are emphasizing the wrong word in a sentence, they will *read or say* the line how it should be said.

This would happen many times to me when I was starting out. It wasn't my favorite thing to hear but you will get used to it.

If you never get a note or a line reading from a director, count your blessings - you are doing it right.

NOTHING PERSONAL

Get used to the idea that when you are on stage, you are playing a character and not yourself. Your character may say or do things that you would never say or do. One of the joys of acting is that it gives you the freedom and permission to alter your mind. You may be playing a deranged ax murderer, a Druid Ninja or a mutant oak tree - where else can you get away with this behavior without being arrested or committed to an institution? Don't let who YOU are - get in the way of who your character is. A character is nothing personal.

PART 4

THE FLOW OF
A SHOW

KNOW ABOUT FLOW

B efore I go much further, I want to introduce the concept of "flow" during a performance, because "flow" plays an important role in surviving on stage. Simply put, 'flow' is a play moving along without distractions or interruptions.

An actor experiences "flow" when their confidence and concentration is solid - this can also be called being "in character" or even being "in the moment". For anyone new to the stage; it's similar to reading a book, watching a movie or listening to music – you become so involved that you're not aware of anything else. Your concentration is absorbed in the book, movie or music and you are in the flow of the story or the music.

Now imagine, someone walks up and asks you a question or just begins talking to you. Your concentration is now broken and the flow is interrupted. You are yanked back into reality. The same principle can happen to actors on the stage when someone says the wrong line, forgets a line, misses an entrance or any number of things.

Side Note: The audience also can become involved in a play and the same disruptions can take them right out of the flow as well.

Another way to define "flow" is everything moving forward in a play from the moment the first line is spoken to the final line. Everything that is *supposed* to happen. Flow should not be confused with "pace". Pace is the how quickly or slowly the play moves from beginning to end. Flow can affect the pace of a play. If the flow is broken for whatever reason, the pace can be altered by speeding up or slowing down.

How Do I Learn the Flow?

(Flow Learners)

You learn the flow of play by doing it over and over again during the rehearsals. When you repeat the same action over and over, you tend to get familiar with it.

Example:

20 times you've walked on stage and said the line:

"I've come to pick up the package."

And 20 times the other actor replied:

"The package is there on the table."

The 21st time you walk on stage and say-

"I've come to pick up the package."

The other actor replies,

"Aunt Bunny! Lovely to see you! Where are the kittens?"

There was a certain routine you experienced 20 times before and now this time it's different. The flow is broken. There is no package, only kittens. Of course, if you recall in the earlier section about improvisation, you should think - *yes and* - instead of saying to the actor, *there are no kittens and my name is not Aunt Bunny.*

❅ ❅ ❅

FLOW BREAKERS

There are many things that can disrupt the flow of a play such as an actor saying the wrong line at the wrong time or not saying anything. One of the main causes of things going wrong on stage is being nervous in front of an audience.

There is something about being in front of a crowd of people that can cause your system to kick into a defensive mode of "fight or flight" and adrenaline is released into your system. This release of adrenaline gives you tremendous energy to either do battle or run away quickly, but you are an actor in play, beating up the audience or running away would upset many people, namely the director, so instead you will just be "nervous."

When you are nervous your heart will pound, your hands may shake, perhaps your mouth goes dry, your mind can race with a thousand thoughts or worse not produce a single thought. Being nervous uses up a lot of energy which is a lot of work and all that work makes it hard to concentrate and remember things - such as lines.

So, what makes us nervous?

THE NERVE BARRIER

S ome 1st-time actors tend to equate *acting* on stage with public speaking. In one sense, an actor is *speaking* in public, but that 's where the similarity ends.

Public speaking is facing a group of people and.. well, speaking or giving a speech to the public. When you're giving a speech, you are not a character in a play, you are yourself in reality. Needless to say, the thought of speaking in front of people can make some uneasy or even nervous.

An interesting fact about public speaking is that people tend to feel more secure when speaking behind a podium or desk. Studies have shown that many amateur speakers felt less nervous when there was an 'object' between themselves and the public. Psychologically, an object, such as a podium or desk represents a "barrier" or a symbol of protection.

If the audience decided to attack during a speech, there is a safe place to hide. Of course, I am joking but actually not far from the truth. In the old days, if an audience didn't care for your speech, they would throw tomatoes or other assorted fruit and vegetation. While a podium was invented as a nice place to hold papers and other objects, it also served as a great vegetable bunker.

O.K. so public speakers have podiums and desks, what does an actor have? What barrier do they have between themselves and the audience? A great one called "a character".

A character is a great hiding place in which an actor can disappear; an organic podium you can hide behind. Nerves come into play when you think about people watching you and you believe these people may be judging you for what you do and what you say. But once again, let me point out it's the character that is 'doing' and 'saying' things, not you.

The fact is, it's very natural to be nervous right before you go on stage. However, you will find that once you step foot on stage and become part of the play and blend into the flow, your mind doesn't have time to realize how nervous you are. It's too busy recalling the lines and blocking that you've memorized. As you are absorbed into the flow of the play, all the thoughts that made you nervous are pushed to the back of your mind and the adrenaline that is left flowing through your system, is pure energy.

COMFORT FOOD
FOR THOUGHT

E xperience has taught me, that how nervous I am before a show - is directly proportional to how secure I am in knowing my lines. If I don't feel secure with my lines, then my nervousness is doubled.

Also, other actors can influence your comfort level - someone who has gone blank a few times or jumps around in the script, it's doubtful that you will feel comfortable with them on stage.

The key here is comfort. You feel comfortable when you know your lines and are reasonably sure the other actors do as well. Fear produces nervousness and of course, fear is bred by the unknown. You can eliminate fear by eliminating the unknown.

If you don't know your lines, learn them. Then you can relax.

How Can I Relax?

Most of the actors I've known have a set routine to help them relax prior to a performance. Along with doing vocal exercises to warm up their voices, they will also loosen their muscles by stretching or even incorporating yoga routines. Some actors find a quiet dark place to be alone while others channel their nervousness into insane energy and jump around like a 6-year-old who just consumed a ton of sugar.

Clear the Fear

One way to tame any fear you may have is to increase your confidence in your lines and role. How? Try running the play and your lines over and over until you can do it in your sleep. The more confidence you have, the less room your mind has for fear.

Feeling relaxed on stage is important because if you're "freaking out" from the beginning and someone else goes blank or jumps 20 pages ahead, your panic level can fly off the charts. You may melt down and run screaming from the stage. And we know running and screaming will upstage everyone. But hey, you'll get noticed.

But seriously, the point is that the more relaxed and comfortable you are, the easier it is for your mind to think of a solution if the flow is interrupted.

CAN YOU SEE IT?

When you are not rehearsing the play with others try rehearsing it by yourself - see the play in your mind. What?

Yes. See the play. There is a technique used by famous people and especially athletes, called "visualization". Before an athlete takes the field, they visualize themselves in the game. A baseball pitcher may mentally see himself keeping the ball down. A quarterback will imagine himself dropping back and throwing a perfect pass. It's essentially a "mental" rehearsal.

Actors also can visualize themselves on stage, saying every line, conveying every emotion from the beginning to the end.

If you think about it, a rehearsal is nothing more than a live visualization. It's not the actual play being performed before a live audience, it's merely the director and everyone visualizing how it should look, the pace and it should have.

I personally have used "visualization" a few times to help me get a feeling for my character and surroundings. In college, I did a play where the set was "representational" - meaning the set did not actually have flats to represent walls.

Novice note: a "flat" is a large piece of fabric, canvas or other stretched over a large wooden frame. They are propped up to create the walls or other parts of a set.

The stage was bare with only a few set pieces such as a few tables and a counter, There was a door frame and a window frame suspended from the ceiling to represent, well... a door and a window. The rest of the stage was surrounded by black curtains.

This bare set was supposed to "represent" an old drug store in Brooklyn, so to help me get a feeling for it, I would come in early before rehearsals and walk around the empty space and visualize what it might look like in reality. I imagined what the walls would look like, old and dirty, with advertisements hanging on them. I pictured the drug store shelves and what items would be stocked there. What the floor would like etc.. Just visualizing those features made me feel very comfortable on stage. And when I was comfortable on the stage, I was relaxed.

Over and Over

Depending on your particular group and director, re-hearsals can be widely varied in time and structure. At first, there is a lot of 'busy work' going on besides your lines and blocking, you will be trying on costumes and makeup, and maybe set construction. But as you get closer to opening night you begin running through the play without distractions and without the script in your hand., you will begin working with "props" you may have to use on stage.

Novice Note: A "Prop" (short for Property) is an object you have to hold or use. A glass of water, a gun etc..

It goes without saying that if you're still holding your script, it makes it difficult to work with props.

Types Of Rehearsals

My favorite directors would run the play straight through without unnecessary stops. Notes were given at the end of the rehearsal. Yes, Notes.

Novice Note: Directors will make notes to give the cast during rehearsals. Notes such as: "come in earlier when you say this line" or "look more amused when you open the door" More than likely you will be 'off book' and cannot write these notes down, you will have to remember them.

Non-Stop Type

A non-stop rehearsal gives you a good feeling of how the show moves, and where it stalls. If anyone takes a long pause before giving a line, everyone knows it. If anyone misses and entrance or a line, everyone knows it. To tell you the truth, you may eventually get bored with rehearsals. But actually ,that is a good thing! If you are "bored" it means you know the show backward and forwards, inside and out. Your comfort level and confidence must be very secure to allow boredom to creep in. Personally, I don't feel comfortable going 'live' until I feel completely bored with it. If you feel bored with rehearsals, chances are you are ready.

Stop and Start Type

There are other directors who are fond of stopping the action and giving notes as you rehearse. Don't get me wrong, notes are important, but I've had directors stop the play every five minutes to give a note. This Red light/Green light approach doesn't give an actor much opportunity to get a feeling of pace or flow. My experience under these conditions was nerve racking. Finally, when we did run the play without stopping, the flow and pace of the show had a stuttering, herky-jerky feeling. Every actor seemed to be unsure if it was O.K. to continue, as if they were waiting for the director to shout from the audience, "No! Wait! Do it this way!"

Time and Place

You may have a limited rehearsal schedule, for example;. I've been in some plays where the rehearsals were only two nights a week for a month. I've been in rehearsals that were held in basements, churches and living rooms. The cast didn't step foot on the actual stage of the theatre until a day or two before opening night. You had to adapt your blocking very quickly, because that long DS cross you'd been rehearsing in the basement turns out to be 3 short steps on the stage. Also, you must quickly adapt to lighting and black outs. There is nothing like act one ending and you're in complete darkness trying to find your way offstage to exit along with everyone else. The key to all of this is the fact that you must be ready to adapt to anything.

RULE 9: Adapt to Anything and Everything

As I stated previously, once you know the flow of a play which includes knowing your lines, blocking, cues and have a good idea what other actors going to do and say and you are feeling comfortable in rehearsals almost to the point of boredom, I can introduce events that you must adapt to in order to keep the flow of the play moving.

Click Click You're Dead

Allow me to share an example of my first experience with the flow of a play being interrupted. I was in a play called "The Gazebo" in High School. The plot of this play revolves around the main character, (played by yours truly), believing he has shot someone and the comic consequences that follow.

During a live performance, we arrived at the crucial "shooting" scene and the prop gun, (a starter pistol that we borrowed from the track team), did not fire. Nothing. Nada. I squeezed off five or six audible 'clicks' without a single sound resembling a gunshot. The actor playing the shooting victim wasn't sure what to do, so - just as he had always done in rehearsals, clutched his chest and fell forward. Normally, this was a dramatic scene, but this time it was met with uproarious laughter.

(**novice note**: audiences love it when mistakes are obvious on stage.)

In the very next scene, an actor missed his entrance cue on stage. I projected my line (his cue) with adequate volume, turned toward the door expecting to see him enter as usual...nothing. Nada.

NOTE: Normally, if someone doesn't enter when are supposed to, the rule is - the other actors 'cover' the mistake by making up dialogue or ad libbing until the late actor comes on stage. Well, that a good rule but the problem was, I was alone on stage, so ad libbing with someone else was not an option. In order to keep the flow moving forward, I walked over and picked up a prop telephone and ad libbed a phone call.

But wait, there's more! Toward the end of the show, an unsecured piece of scenery fell over onto the main set with a tremendous crash and you guessed it, more laughter from the audience.

As I previously stated, flow is 'everything that is *supposed* to happen' during a performance. None of these events were *supposed* to happen, therefore, all sense of flow, went right out the window. Actually, *flow* opened the window and fled right after the first 'click' of the prop gun.

You may have heard the expression; "*The Show Must Go On*" - which means exactly what it says. No matter whathappens on stage, the show *must* and *will* continue moving foward. If you go blank, or someone else goes blank, or scenery falls down, or an actor falls down, it does not matter--it's a ball rolling down a hill. I was in a play where an actress was injured during a scene but the show did not stop. I had a slight case of pneumonia with 103 temperature on the opening night of play--my doctor said to stay in bed, but doctor, you don't understand, the show must go on. I went on. Sure, my performance was a bit wonky, but I had to do it. There was no understudy.

Note: An *Understudy* is another actor who can re-place at the main actor in the case of illness or other reasons.

SIDE EFFECTS

O nce the flow of a play is interrupted by a major mistake or blooper, an actor can find it difficult to 'stay in character' and get the flow back on track. As the prop gun clicked with a bang , it wasn't the *character* in the play who panicked, it was the *actor* in the character who did. Unfortunately, as a side effect - the panic spread to the rest of the cast and created a domino effect.

 The actor who missed his entrance was deeply engaged in a discussion backstage on the unfortunate state of prop guns not firing and was not listening for his cue.

Another actor who was distracted by what was happening (or not happening), realized he forgot to set a prop on the other side of the stage, which he normally did at intermission He decided to sneak behind the scenery, as the play was going on, to place his prop. About the time he discovered the path behind the scenery was too narrow, he bumped into it, causing it to topple over onto the set.

So the truth of the matter is - you don't even have to be on stage to upset the flow of a play. You can cause chaos behind the scenes.

It's not always the case where one thing goes wrong that everything else will go wrong, the point is; if the flow is disrupted in a major way, an actors concentration can also be disrupted. When concentration is absent, mistakes have room to take over.

Here again- "The show must go on". That is one steadfast rule you will learn and that is to keep moving forward by adapting to whatever happens. (Unless, someone dies on stage -which has happened- and in that case, the show must Not go on.)

But just like the actor who went ahead and clutched his chest and fell forward even though the prop gun didn't fire - he kept the flow of the scene moving. I improvised a telephone call to keep the flow going when the other actor missed his entrance.

Sometimes you must adapt by doing or saying something that is "not" supposed to happen to keep the flow going.

RULE 10: "Keep the flow for those who don't know" .

As I said: try to have a good idea of the other actor's lines and movements. I am not suggesting that you memorize everyone's role, it's just a good idea to generally know *what* they are supposed to say and *when* they are supposed to say it.

A benefit of rehearsing a play over and over is that you will become familiar with lines and blocking that are not your own. You will know when other actors are supposed to enter and exit, when the wind should blow the candle out etc...

Even if you have a small part with one line, you will become familiar with more than your line. It's like hearing a song over and over on the radio, after a while, you can't help but know all the words. Knowing another actor's lines can save the day.

In the good old days of theatre, if an actor went blank on stage, he could rely on a person called a "prompter". The prompter was hidden in a small alcove at the very front of the stage. You will sometimes see these little boxes in front of the stage in very old theatrers. The prompter could whisper out lines if an actor went blank. On the amateur stage, a prompter is a rarely used, therefore, actors only have each other to rely upon.

WHAT TO DO
IF SOMEONE
GOES BLANK?

I f another actor goes blank on stage, (also called 'going up' 'going south' 'blanking") , and you know what they are supposed to say - one of the best methods to prompt them is by asking a question or making a statement that contains a clue to their line.

Example:

If you know the other actor's line is supposed to be:

"I came here to review the bank receipts."

You can help with a simple prompt such as:

Question: *"Are you here to review the bank receipts?"*
or

Statement: *"I need someone to review these bank re-*

ceipts"

The trick is to adapt the other actor's line and make it sound like one of your own. This keeps the flow moving.

I have stood on stage in complete silence with other actors who will only say their *own* lines. If it's not *their* line, they will remain silent. They could help by prompting you, but won't. In some cases, there is no help. Nothing anyone can say will prompt you.

I heard a story of an actor who went blank on stage and other actors attempted to help by feeding him prompts such as, "Weren't you going to tell us about your wife dying?" The struggling actor would actually wave off any help saying to the others, "I'll get it! I'll remember it in a minute! Leave me alone!" According to this story, this went on for almost 10 minutes.

Note: If someone is trying to help you, **by all means, take it!**

I have had this happen on stage where there was suddenly silence in the scene I was in. There were only two of us on stage at the time and I was positive the other actor's line was "How is your son? Is he doing well?" I was sure that is what he was supposed to ask but he didn't.

So, I used the *question trick* and asked the actor - "I suppose you are wondering about my son?" *(to cue him)*

 He looked at me for a second and said, "Nope."

The issue in the scene was - I had another line and

I did not say it. My mind drifted - I lost the flow and thought it was his line - but it was my line. Unfortunately, he did not think "yes and" - picking it up from that spot, he deny it.

Adapting is very important. Refusing to adapt and prompting an actor who has gone blank because it's not your line is a tad selfish as well as, ignoring the help of other others actors who are trying to help you. Adapt to help. Don't deny.

ADAPT FAIL

I was in a play where an actor missed his entrance. Fortunately, this time, I was not alone on stage, so per the rule - the other actors including myself ad-libbed for a bit to cover.

After a few minutes, it became obvious we couldn't keep going until he entered the scene, otherwise, we would have made up a whole new scene and maybe a whole new play.

One of the actors suddenly said, "*You know what? I need to ask Joe something. Hey Joe! Could you come out here for a minute!*" And after a little hesitation, the actor playing Joe finally made his entrance and the scene continued as it was supposed to.

After the play ended, we were in the dressing rooms and someone asked the actor playing Joe, "*So what happened? Why didn't you enter?*" The actor playing Joe replied, "*You didn't say my cue line.*" Another older actor spoke up and said, "*So what does it matter? You know you're supposed to enter! So enter! Whether he says your cue or he sneezes, farts, coughs or sings Happy Birthday, get your ass out there!"*

The point is, no matter if your cue is a line, a sound or a rocket going off , you know where it is - in the flow of a scene - be prepared to adjust and/or adapt if it doesn't happen. Keep the flow moving.

What If I Forget?

If you forget your line and are left floating in a sea of silence with no help and you have knots in your stomach, relax, there are a few things you can do.

If you go blank, take a moment and mentally replay the cue or repeat the line that was just said and this can prompt you. This method has worked for me quite a few times. I had a short monologue in a one-act play and around the middle of it, I reached the end of one of my lines and the next line was not there to meet me. I paused, (as if I was supposed to) and played back the last few lines in my mind and tah-dah! I remembered the next line and was able to continue. When this happens, hopefully it never does for you, be aware that one second of silence to an actor feels like one minute. Two seconds feels like an hour.

* * *

WORKING OUT THE KINKS IN REHEARSALS

Ideally, the best time to work through mistakes and/or forget your lines is during the final rehearsals before opening night. In most cases, a director will run the entire play from start to finish without allowing the actors to "call" for a line

. (**Novice Note:** "Calling for a line" simply means when you go blank you call out, "line?" And someone who is following along in the script will help you out.)

During the final few rehearsals, the director will simply let the actors struggle through the play; if they go blank, miss an entrance or forget a prop, well then, so be it. It's during this time you will discover where your weakness may be - in remembering lines or movements as well as where others may be weak. Personally, those final rehearsals really help me to learn where I need to improve. I will go back to the script and run those weak spots over and over until I get them.

If you do go blank in front of an audience or something goes wrong, it's important not to let it show. The way an actor lets it show is called *breaking character*.

Breaking out

I previously talked about being "in-character", which is *you* the character, not *you* the actor. This leads me to the rule about "**staying in-character**". That is, not allowing *you* the *actor* to poke your head out of *you* the *character*.

In the example I gave about the actor who went blank on stage and refused help from his fellow actors - when he said; "I'll get it! I'll remember it in a minute! Leave me alone!" - this was the actor speaking, not the character in the play.

When you speak as yourself, you are "breaking character". When you "break" character, you are breaking the flow. It could be said that *breaking character* is doing or saying something not as the character but as yourself.

If you allow the audience to recognize you the actor, you are "breaking" character. A visual for this would be near the end of the film **The Wizard of Oz**, when Toto pulls back the curtain and reveals that the Wizard is just a man pushing buttons and pulling levers. As an actor, you are behind a curtain called a character.

When you are on stage and in-character, stay behind the curtain and keep little dogs away.

RULE 11 : Stay In Character

SUSPENDING DISBELIEF

When we are watching a play, movie or a TV show, on a real world level, we know that what we are seeing is not actually happening. (hopefully we know)

We are completely aware that we're watching actors who are saying lines that were written in a script. Having said that, at the same time, on another level of our brain, (the imagination level) we play along. We allow ourselves to ignore reality, and we do this by 'suspending disbelief'.

For a time, we will imagine there is someone named Bruce Wayne who goes out dressed as Batman and fights crime in a place called Gotham City or that there is a place called Middle Earth where Hobbits and Dwarves dwell. A teenager named Romeo is truly in love with Juliet. We can even get emotionally caught up in the story and react to it as if it's all true. We can laugh at an awkward situation, become extremely tense during a suspenseful moment, and even cry when a character dies.

In much the same way an actor must concentrate to remain in character, the audience requires a certain amount of concentration to suspending their disbelief.

No matter how far an audience is willing to ignore reality, once they do, your job as an actor is keep them there.

When an actor breaks character, chances are good the suspension of disbelief of the audience will also break.

Why?

When an actor breaks character, they are reminding the audience of the reality that they were comfortably ignoring. Once this happens, it's very can be difficult to ease them back into their suspension.

Take me Out

There is an expression; "taken out of it" -which is used when someone is suddenly snapped back into reality. It happens to me when I see bad special effects or plot twists that twist way too far. Anytime you're watching something and find yourself saying "Oh Come On!" You have been "taken out of it".

It will not always be the actor's fault if the audience is "taken out of it". In my high school horror story about the prop gun not firing and the scenery falling, these events took the audience (and actors) out of it.

The trick to getting the audience back in it, is to keep the flow going. Despite anything that is *not* supposed to happen, if you keep moving forward with everything else that *is* supposed to happen, you will allow the audience an opportunity to get their suspenders back out and hang up their disbelief.

WHAT THEY DON'T KNOW WON'T HURT YOU

It really depends on the seriousness of the *mistake* that happens during a play which will determine whether to ignore it or adjust to it.

Example:

If an actor skips a word or says the wrong word in his line, no one will notice. (you can keep going)

If an actor skips a whole line, maybe a few will notice. (you may have to adjust a little)

If an actor skips his entrance, quite a few people will notice. (you will have to adapt)

Remember, in most cases, the audience doesn't know the play as well as the actors. They won't be aware of any small mistakes during the show.

If you need to adjust or adapt to a mistake, one of the best ways is to acknowledge it in character.

Examples:

A picture hanging on the set falls on the stage - an actor adapts by saying; "Oh that picture fell again! That's the third time this year!"

An actor accidentally trips as he enters the stage - he adapts by adding: "I've got to fix that loose floor board! Somebody could fall!"

You can cover some mistakes by acknowledging it in character and adapting your dialogue to fit the situation. The idea is to make something that *wasn't* supposed o happen, seem as though it *was* supposed to happen. This will keep the audience with you and keep the flow moving.

What They Do Know Can Hurt You

One of the biggest mistakes an actor can make is trying to ignore something that falls on the stage. Some actors believe if they aren't looking at it, the audience won't look at it.

Quite the opposite is true. If anything falls on the stage, an actress's ear ring pops off, an actor's button, a feather from a boa, anything - the audiences attention will focus on it. (Remember my side note about how the audience loves obvious mistakes?)

Mostly the crowd will be curious to see if someone will pick it up. If you drop something in real life it's only natural to pick it up.

RULE 11: If it falls, pick it up.

You don't know how many times I've seen novice actors being yelled at backstage by a director or other actors, "Why didn't you pick it up?! If it falls, pick it up!"

Remember: <u>adapt.</u>

Most first time freeze up on stage if any variable occurs during play. We didn't rehearse this! Buttons pop off, glasses and cups get knocked over, pens and pencils roll off a tables, the laws of physics are not suspended on the stage. Things happen. Just because it's not written in the margin of your script as blocking, doesn't mean it didnt happen.

WHEN NOT TO ACKNOWLEDGE MISTAKES

I was in a production where I had a page of dialogue about a bag of pretzels. The actress who brought the pretzel bag out to me, walked on stage empty handed. I looked at her with a hint of panic in my eye. She shrugged as if to say, "Oh well." (apparently, the pretzel bag was not on the prop table)

Without missing a beat, the actress skipped ahead in the script to the section just beyond my lines about the pretzels. We continued on as if nothing happened.

To B or Not
Sometimes it helps to consider the flow of a play moving forward; A to B to C. A (the beginning) B (the middle) and C (the end). This gives you a simple struc-

ture or formula to visualize. You know you have to go through A to get to B and so forth. Now imagine each scene within a play having that same A-B-C pattern. A: You enter a scene. B: You walk around and say some lines and finally C: You exit or the subject of the scene changes or moves on to something else.

I worked with a director who would divide the scenes of a play up into a similar pattern she called "French Scenes".

French scenes are a way to split up the scenes based the characters present. For example, if a scene has 3 characters on stage and one of the characters exit, that is a french scene. It's not necessarily the end of that scene, it's just the end of those 3 characters being on stage. Now there are 2 characters on stage that is a new French Scene.

The A-to-B-to-C flow is similar but it focuses on the "subject" of a scene. It doesn't matter how many characters are on stage but considers what the characters are talking about. There could be multiple subjects in a scene or just one.

If an actor thinks of a scene in the A-to-B-to-C pattern, it can help if something goes wrong with the flow. You know that you start at A, go through B to get to C. Much in the same way that you leave home (A) and need to get to work or school (C), but maybe there's an accident or detour, so you need to alter your path (B) to get there. You have to adjust B. You can think of acting in a scene the same way - as an example:

In the pretzel bag scene I illustrated earlier using the A-B-C structure:

A: We enter the scene.

B: The actress hands me a pretzel bag and we talk. (subject = Pretzel Bag)

C: I stop talking about the Pretzels and the subject moves on to the next.

That's how it's supposed to flow.

But now, suddenly, there's a Detour at B = the item (prop) that creates the Subject (Pretzel Bag) is missing.

We started at A, however, when the actress realized the pretzel bag was not there - she knew we could not move on to point B. The subject of point B would make no sense to the audience.

She adapted by skipping ahead to point C, and thereby kept the flow moving to the next subject.

Skipping over B was not obvious to the audience, unless someone was familiar with the play or the playwright was sitting out there, but no one knew the scene took a detour from A to C.

Of course, this little glitch could have been prevented if we had checked our props.

RULE 12: Check Your Props

Simply put -if you have an important prop: a bag of

pretzels, a prop gun, a suitcase etc.. anything that you will need to carry on during a play, make sure it's there before the show begins.

Most theatre groups will have a "prop person" who is in charge of all the items used in the play and usually there may be a "props" table where all the items are kept. It doesn't hurt to make sure everything you need is there.

Developing Bad Habits

As you do the play over and over you may start to notice some odd performances. Now, I'm not speaking of a particular actor's take on a role, (how he or she performed as a character in a play), but more specifically, the strange idiosyncrasies or habits a particular actor gave to a character that had nothing really to do with the play or role itself.

For example, I had a minor role in a community theatre production of a play called *"Night Watch"*. One of the other actors had the most unusual way of carrying himself around the stage - the best way I can describe it is... that he looked like a marionette, you know, a creepy puppet whose movements were guided by strings. When we were in rehearsals, or in common daily interaction, the guy was quite normal. He walked around with no unusual flair. But when the house lights went down and the stage lights went up - some mystical transformation occurred when he made his entrance.

When he walked from stage left to stage right, it was as if invisible strings were pulling at legs, enabling his movement. It gave him this faux like marching action as if he were carefully prancing through a mind field. Why didn't the director say something? Did the role call for this weird gait? Was it a brave performance choice to give his character depth. Was this just a bad habit the actor started and now couldn't change? I have no idea.

I said something to one of the other actors, such as: "Is it me or does Rick look like crazed marionette performing 'March of the Wooden Soldiers'?" They all agreed and someone responded, "He just thinks he's acting."

Over the years that phrase, "He just thinks he's acting" has explained a lot of oddball performances. Call back to earlier in this book when I noted actors who use British or New York accents for now reason. They think that's acting. No, it's a bad habit.

Over the years I encountered many other types who had strange acting habits. Here are a few:

Squatters - Several actors I knew who would slightly squat down when speaking a line.

Leaners -   They lean slightly forward when delivering a line as if they are about to bow.

Blinkers or **Blind acting** - those who blink rapidly or completely close their eyes when delivering a line - my theory is- they are mentally picturing the script and reading their lines.

Look Away - a variation of eye blinking/closers who stare at something off to the left or right or a few feet above your head.

Big Actors (Over The Top style) - Actors who make every word and action very big and overly dramatic. This trait is usually instilled in some actors at an early age, whether beauty pageants refugees or high school theatre directors who keep telling the actors "Make it Bigger! Bigger!" as if every play is actually a Melodrama and you must command the stage like Ethyl Merman belting out a showstopper.

Iambic Actors - actors who deliver every line with a poetic cadence as if they are reciting a sonnet. (we covered those guys)

While many of these traits are bad habits that were learned or taught, many of them are derived from some inner perception of what it is to perform. Unfortunately, this inner perception is actually a misconception

As I noted earlier, I had a habit of swallowing the end of my lines. My overall volume would drop off near the last few words of a line and honestly, I was unaware that I was doing it.

Sometimes it only takes someone, a director or fellow actor to point out a bad habit to correct it. All those years ago if someone would have approached the "marionette" guy and say "Hey, not sure if you were aware, but you're walking very oddly on stage." If may have helped or it may not have. The actor who used a British accent in every role never changed it.

The lesson here is simple - take all the preconceived notions you have about acting and keep them open to change. Most of them may be bad habits or misguided instructions you received early in your career. The mental scripts you have in your mind may not always work for the play scripts you have in your hand. If you stand up straight and deliver a line as opposed to squatting or leaning, won't alter your overall performance. Keep what you "think" is "acting" open to change.

GOING LIVE WITH LAUGHS OR THE ROAR OF THE CROWD

I f you are in comedy play and it's your first time on stage, you may become of aware of a strange sound coming from the audience - laughter. When you are running through the play in rehearsals, you're aware of the funny moments and witty dialogue, but the repetition of rehearsing wears the funniness away and you can almost forget that the play is a comedy.

An important rule about comedy is to remember it's funny and allow time for the laughs.

RULE 13: Wait for the Laughs.

This rule can get technical because comedy has this complex feature known as "timing". If an actor says a funny line, and doesn't allow time for the audience to laugh, but instead goes right into the next line; he or she will teach the crowd a bad habit. That bad habit is not to laugh as much or at all for the next funny line.

Why?

Well, if an actor tries to deliver lines while the audience is laughing, they will stop laughing so that they can hear what is being said. The crowd quickly adapts to the timing of the actors and learns early on that they might miss something important that is being said on stage and will stop laughing.

The trick of successful comedy on stage is to discover the timing of mass laughter. Consider it like this: a large group of people laughing at the same time is really just one big sound - it starts off soft and gets louder, it rises to a peak and then comes back down.

 The timing trick is to wait for the laughter to reach its peak and as it begins to decline, (about halfway down) it's safe to continue.

The rule is to come in a tad bit louder than usual, so the audience can hear you.

And finally - the last rule of being on stage and perhaps the most important is to have fun!

RULE 14: Have Fun.

Almost every director I have ever worked with has included statement as a final note to the cast; "Have fun!"

After all, if you think about it, being on a stage under the lights, in a costume and pretending to be a different person is a lot of fun. There is nothing like having the audience hanging onto your every word in a dramatic scene or hearing the crowd laughing at something you said and best of all, there is nothing like hearing applause at the end of a play.

Acting in theatrical performance is very hard work. As you have learned, there are quite a few rules you must remember, not to mention lines of dialogue and blocking you have to recall. There are hours of free time you have to give up to just to be in a play and certainly there will be more rules and guidelines you will learn along the way. Enjoy your journey.

✳ ✳ ✳

ABOUT THE AUTHOR

Lee Mueller

Lee Mueller was born in St. Louis, Missouri. For over thirty years he has been involved in the performing arts, from acting, directing, improv/ sketch comedy, and most notably as a playwright. His first one-act play, "In Between Days" was selected to be produced during a national writers conference at a local Missouri College. His second one-act, "The Favor" was chosen as a finalist in a short play competition by Pamoja Players in St. Louis.

For over 20 years, Lee has specialized in comedy murder mystery plays that have been produced all over the world. His play "Death Of A Doornail" won "Best Original Comedy" at the 27th Annual "Arty Awards" in Fairfield California.

BOOKS BY THIS AUTHOR

A Medley Of Murder Mystery Plays (Volume 1)

3 comedy murder mystery plays by Lee Mueller. A collection of earliest play scripts and some of his most popular works that have been produced nationally and internationally. This medley of mystery includes "Murder Me Always" - During a very bad performance of "Murder Me Always", a real murder takes place off stage. The Director is shot. The "fake" play comes to a halt and a "real" murder mystery begins.
"Talk About A Murder" - A Television talk Show is taping a live broadcast. One of the guests turns up dead, while the show is "live" on the air. Can the hosts and guests solve the murder? Will it boost their ratings? Must the Show go on?
And the award-winning "Death Of A Doornail" - An eccentric Millionaire, Albert Doornale has invited all of his close friends to his estate. Only problem is, Albert is missing. No one has seen him. Was Albert killed? Kidnapped? A murder investigation will begin,

as soon as a body is found

A Series Of Short (Serious) Plays

A far cry from Comedic Murder mysteries this is a selection of 5 short play scripts. Plays that range from political to absurd. From the award-winning, "The Thing That Happened" to his most recent play, "Loren Ipsum (sonata for 2 actors)". If you are a fan of his Murder Mystery plays and wondered if his imagination wrought anything but who-dun-its, this is definitely your answer

Idle Essence : Tales Of Marvin - A Collection Of Short Stories

In this collection of short stories and novellas, Lee Mueller examines what it was like growing up in the Midwest in the 1970s through the character of Marvin Milstead. Marvin is an only child left to his own devices, imagination, and idleness. The stories explore different points and events in Marvin's life from the first day of kindergarten with Kitties In The Garden through the divorce of his parents and adapting those changes and being raised by grandparents and a single mother in For A Change. Chocked full of humor and nostalgia set against the backdrop of the Nixon and Ford years.